I CAN BE AN
AUTHOR

By Ray Broekel

Prepared under the direction of Robert Hillerich, Ph.D.

 CHILDRENS PRESS ®

CHICAGO

Library of Congress Cataloging in Publication Data
Broekel, Ray.
  I can be an AUTHOR.
  Includes index.
  Summary: Describes the personal qualities, training,
and tools necessary to be a writer.
  1. Authorship—Vocational guidance—Juvenile
literature. [1. Authorship—Vocational guidance.
2. Vocational guidance. 3. Occupations]
I. Title.
PN153.B76 1986 808'.02   85-28050
ISBN 0-516-01891-4

PICTURE DICTIONARY

newspaper articles

reporter

encyclopedia

interview

fiction

word processor

author

editor

manuscript

Before there were books, storytellers could only tell their stories to a few listeners at a time. But now, through books, they can speak to hundreds of people over many years.

How does a baby let you know how it feels? Sometimes the baby cries. Sometimes the baby smiles or laughs. What is the baby doing? The baby is communicating.

To communicate means to give information to other people. You can communicate by making

author

sounds or signals. Or you can communicate by speaking.

You can also communicate by writing. An author is someone

Everyone has stories to tell. Authors are people who write their stories down for others to read.

whose job is communicating with others by writing. You can communicate with others by becoming an author.

A newspaper reporter spends a lot of time on the phone gathering facts.

newspaper articles

Some authors write nonfiction. Nonfiction is about things that are true or that really happened. Newspaper articles are examples of nonfiction.

This sports writer is writing about a baseball game on a portable computer. He will send the story to his newspaper office through the telephone. Then his story of the game will appear in the morning newspaper.

A reporter is an author who writes newspaper articles. A newspaper article is not a story. It is a report of what, where, why, when, and how something happened.

reporter

interview

Authors may write another kind of article—an article about a certain subject. First they do research to find out about the subject. They may talk to people who know about the subject. This is called interviewing.

Interviewing people is one way newspaper reporters do research for their articles. They must find the people who know the facts about a subject or event.

A good author knows how to use the library for research. The card catalog
tells what books are available and where they are located. The reference
section of the library has encyclopedias and many other sources of information.

Or they may read
about the subject in
magazines, books, or
encyclopedias. These
are called sources. A
good author uses at
least three sources when
writing an article.

encyclopedia

fiction

Some authors write fiction stories. Fiction stories are make-believe. They never really took place, but are made up.

A story is different from

Fiction stories are made up, but the way the characters behave is real.

an article. Most stories
are told from the point
of view of a person, or
character, in the story.
The author needs to
think and talk like that
character.

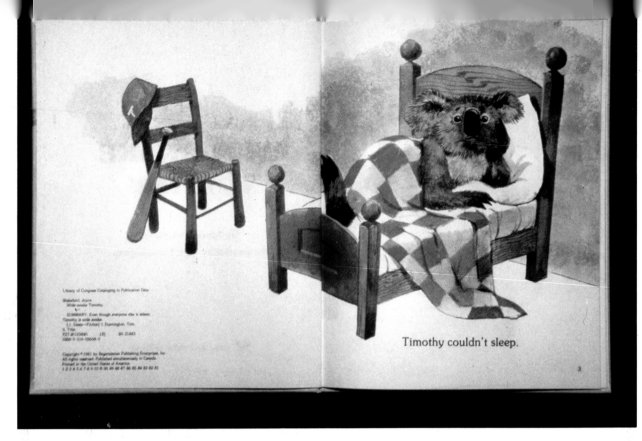

Library of Congress Cataloging in Publication Data

Wakefield, Joyce.
  Wide awake Timothy.

  [SUMMARY: Even though everyone else is asleep,
  Timothy is wide awake.
  [1. Sleep—Fiction] I. Dunnington, Tom.
  II. Title.
  PZ7.W1334Wi   [E]   80-21660
  ISBN 0-516-03656-0

Timothy couldn't sleep.

The main character in this story has a problem.
How do you think he solves his problem?

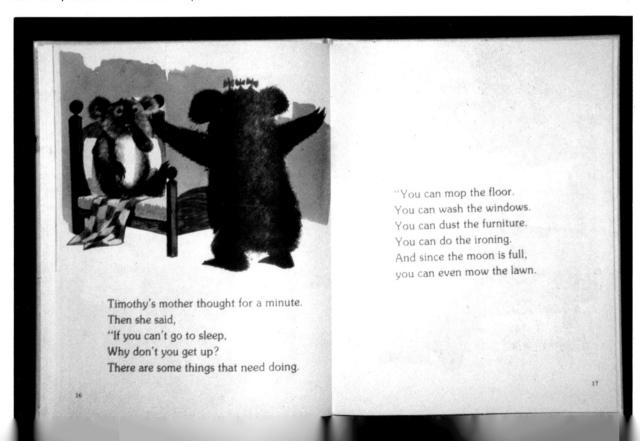

Timothy's mother thought for a minute.
Then she said,
"If you can't go to sleep,
Why don't you get up?
There are some things that need doing.

"You can mop the floor.
You can wash the windows.
You can dust the furniture.
You can do the ironing.
And since the moon is full,
you can even mow the lawn.

A story also has a
conflict, or problem, that
the main character
solves. The conflict may
be a mystery. Or it may
be a simple, everyday
problem such as finding
a way to make friends
with an enemy. The
author must make the
characters in a story act
like real people.

When authors write a whole book, they have a lot more work to do. A book author works about the same way that a writer of stories or articles does. It just takes longer to finish the job.

Some authors work best in a room full of pictures, papers, books, and other favorite objects. Others, like the famous author Ernest Hemingway, prefer "a clean, well-lighted place."

Authors work very hard to make their stories true-to-life and exciting.

Authors spend a lot of time writing. But they spend even more time thinking about their subject. All authors feel that they have something to say. So they look, listen, read, and think. They try to think of the best way to communicate their message to their readers.

Authors often write a story or article by hand first . . .

word processor

manuscript

Finally the author sits down and writes a "first draft." The author may write the draft by hand or type it on a typewriter or a kind of computer called a word processor.

. . .then they type it on a typewriter or word processor.

The next step is revising, or making changes. Authors read their first draft and think about how the story will sound to the people who read it. They try to make it as clear and interesting as possible. They may change some of their words. They may move sentences around.

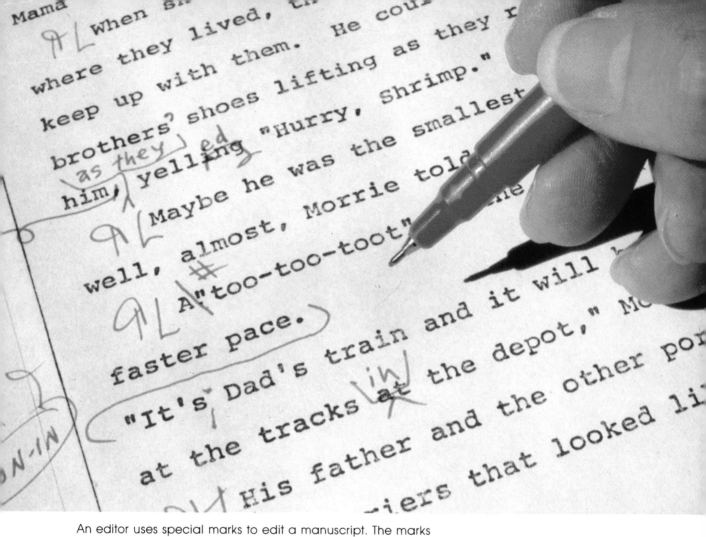

An editor uses special marks to edit a manuscript. The marks tell the typesetter what to do.

Sometimes they move whole sections around. Authors may revise a story four or five times. Each time, it gets better.

Have you read any of these magazines? Your library is
a good place to explore for new things to read.

editor

Soon the final draft, or
manuscript, is finished.
Then the author sends it
to a magazine editor or
a book publisher. The
editor edits the
manuscript, or polishes it
to make it even better.

An author who is working on a story may even keep writing during meals!

An author needs to be a person who gets things done. Writing is not something you can turn on and off. An author needs to write on a regular basis. That is why many authors do some writing each day.

Authors make money by writing. But their best reward is knowing that people enjoy their stories. The author below is signing his name in his books for some admiring fans.

Authors also need self-discipline. Self-discipline means making yourself get down to work. No one forces an author to write. Authors are their own boss. So writing never really gets done unless an author has self-discipline.

Writing is work. But it is also fun. Would you like to be an author?

WORDS YOU SHOULD KNOW

article (AHR • ti • kil)—a piece of nonfiction writing, usually about one subject

character (KAIR • ik • ter)—a person in a story

communicate (kuh • MYOO • ni • kait)—to give information to another person

conflict (KAHN • flikt)—a problem caused by opposite ideas or wants

edit (ED • it)—to improve written material by changing or correcting it

editor (ED • ih • ter)—a person whose job is to edit

encyclopedia (en • sy • klo • PEED • ee • uh)—a book or set of books that gives a lot of information on many subjects

fiction (FIK • shun)—a made-up story

imagination (ih • maj • ih • NAY • shun)—active or creative thinking

information (in • fur • MAY • shun)—facts

interview (IN • tur • vyoo)—to ask questions of a person who knows about some subject

manuscript (MAN • yoo • skript)—a typed or hand-written story or article

mystery (MISS • ter • ee)—something that cannot be understood or that is very hard to figure out.

newspaper (NOOZ • pay • pur)—a printed paper that reports the news

nonfiction (nahn • FIK • shun)—written material about something that is true or that really happened

publisher (PUB • lish • er)—a person or company that produces books, magazines, or newspapers

research (REE • surch)—careful study to collect information about a subject

revise (ree • VYZ)—to correct, change, or improve something

self-discipline (self • DISS • ih • plin)—the ability to make yourself do or not do something

signal (SIG • nul)—a movement or sign that gives a message

source (SOHRSS)—someone or something that supplies information

word processor (WURD PRAH • sess • er)—a kind of computer used for typing, editing, and storing manuscripts, letters, and other documents

INDEX

PHOTO CREDITS

ABOUT THE AUTHOR

Dr. Ray Broekel has written over 1,000 stories and articles for children. He has also written over 150 books on many topics for both children and adults. He has learned that an author needs to go to the right people to find out about a subject. Then he sits down and writes about them.

Dr. Broekel also teaches people how to write. And finally, he has perhaps one of the sweetest hobbies in the world. He is known as the number-one authority in the world on candy bar history.